# American
# NAVAL FORCES
# in the Vietnam War

### AL HEMINGWAY

**WORLD ALMANAC® LIBRARY**

Please visit our web site at: **www.worldalmanaclibrary.com**
For a free color catalog describing World Almanac® Library's list of high-quality books and multimedia programs, call 1-800-848-2928 (USA) or 1-800-387-3178 (Canada). World Almanac® Library's fax: (414) 332-3567.

Library of Congress Cataloging-in-Publication Data

Hemingway, Albert, 1950-
   American naval forces in the Vietnam War / by Al Hemingway.
      p. cm. — (The American experience in Vietnam)
   Includes bibliographical references and index.
   ISBN 0-8368-5776-3 (lib. bdg.)
   ISBN 0-8368-5783-6 (softcover)
   1. Vietnamese Conflict, 1961-1975—Naval operations, American—Juvenile literature.
   2. United States Navy—History—Vietnamese Conflict, 1961-1975—Juvenile literature.
   I. Title. II. Series.
   DS558.7.H45   2005
   959.704'345—dc22                                          2004058095

First published in 2005 by
**World Almanac® Library**
330 West Olive Street, Suite 100
Milwaukee, WI  53212  USA

Developed by Amber Books Ltd.
Editor: James Bennett
Designer: Colin Hawes
Photo research: Natasha Jones
World Almanac® Library editors: Mark Sachner and Alan Wachtel
World Almanac® Library art direction: Tammy West
World Almanac® Library production: Jessica Morris

Picture Acknowledgements
Cody Images (www.codyimages.com): cover (both), 13, 19, 21, 23, 25, 28, 33, 42;
Corbis: 1, 4 (both), 6, 8, 9, 10, 11, 14, 16, 20, 22, 24, 31, 32, 34, 36, 37, 39, 40, 41;
Getty Images: 17; U.S. National Archives: 26.

Printed in Canada

1 2 3 4 5 6 7 8 9 09 08 07 06 05

## About the Author

**AL HEMINGWAY** served in Vietnam with the U.S. Marines in 1969. He was senior editor of *Vietnam Magazine* and has written for *Military History, Modern Warfare, America's Civil War, American Heritage,* and *Leatherneck* magazines. He is the author of *Our War Was Different: U.S. Marine Combined Action Platoons in Vietnam.* He lives in Waterbury, Connecticut.

# Table of Contents

Words that appear in the glossary are printed in **boldface** type the first time they occur in the text

# Introduction

The Vietnam War (1954–1975) was part of a larger conflict known as the Second Indochina War, which raged in Southeast Asia and involved the nations of Cambodia, Laos, and Vietnam. From 1946 until 1954, the Vietnamese had fought for independence from France during the First Indochina War. When the French were defeated, the country was divided into North and South Vietnam. Vietnamese communists controlled North Vietnam and wanted to unify Vietnam under communist rule. Non-communist Vietnamese controlled the South. In the 1950s, the United States and the Soviet Union were in the early years of their struggle over political, economic, and military influence in various parts of the world. Known as the Cold War, this struggle often did not pit each nation against the other directly. Rather, each supported other countries that were squared off against one another. In the mid-1950s, the U.S. began training South Vietnam's army, while the Soviet Union and China backed communist North Vietnam. By the mid-1960s, U.S. forces fought alongside the Army of the Republic of Vietnam (ARVN) against the North Vietnamese Army (NVA) and the National Front for the Liberation of Vietnam (NLF).

The U.S. Navy and Marine Corps performed key roles in Vietnam. In addition to their traditional tasks, however, these branches had to adapt to fight a different kind of war—a war in which the terrain and waterways were unlike anything they had encountered in previous conflicts.

At the outset, the U.S. Navy dispatched aircraft carrier groups and cruiser-destroyer groups off the coast of North and South Vietnam. Air squadrons from the carriers provided close-air support for ground combat troops and bombed targets. The carriers, destroyers, and the USS *New Jersey,* the only battleship to see action during the conflict, supported the infantry with naval gunfire. Smaller boats were quickly built to interrupt the enemy's supply lines coming into South Vietnam. Prior to the Vietnam War, the U.S. Navy had no attack-helicopter squadrons. That changed with the arrival of the Seawolves. These UH–1B Huey gunships supported the riverboats and naval commandos on their raids.

The U.S. Marine Corps, which fought on land and in the sea and air, also faced tremendous challenges in Vietnam. From 1965 until 1971, they deployed twenty-four infantry **battalions**, ten battalions of **artillery**, two tank battalions, two antitank battalions, three amphibious tractor battalions, two reconnaissance battalions, twenty-six flying squadrons, and numerous logistical and support units. The Marines' traditional role had been to attack the enemy from the sea, but now Marines found themselves fighting the NVA and communist **guerrilla** fighters known as the Viet Cong (VC) in the jungles and cities of South Vietnam. In 1968, Marines drove NVA and VC forces out of Hue City and defended their combat base at Khe Sanh against a seventy-seven day siege while being pounded by NVA artillery. The Marines also organized the Combined Action Program in which squads lived in South Vietnamese villages and trained the people to defend their homes.

**Below:** This map shows North and South Vietnam and the surrounding area. Key regions, cities, and military bases are indicated.

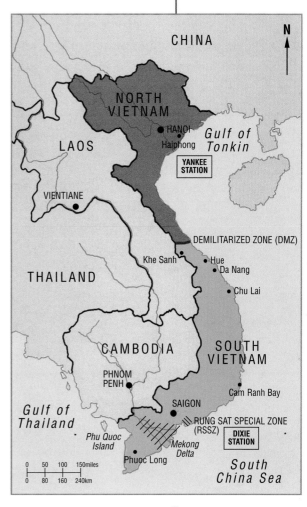

# The Navy at Sea

**Right:** The aircraft carrier USS *Constellation* was deployed seven times in Southeast Asia. Aircraft from carriers struck enemy targets in North Vietnam and provided close air support for ground troops.

The U.S. Navy had a major role in the Vietnam War. Its involvement began with the Gulf of Tonkin incident in 1964, and continued until the fall of South Vietnam in 1975. Navy pilots, and the crews of aircraft carriers, cruisers, and destroyers, all had their roles to play in fighting the war.

## AIRCRAFT CARRIERS

Aircraft carriers operated from two areas off the coast of Vietnam: Dixie Station and Yankee Station. Dixie Station was about 75 miles (120 kilometers) southeast of Saigon, the capital of South Vietnam. From here, planes based on aircraft carriers provided close-air support for ground troops and bombed targets in South Vietnam. Yankee Station was situated hundreds of miles north. Aircraft conducted operations against North Vietnam from this location.

Yankee Station was by far the most dangerous. In the skies over North Vietnam, naval pilots had to face surface-to-air missiles (SAMs) and antiaircraft fire, known as flak. Planes sometimes limped back to their ships full of holes caused by the flak.

Seaman Roland Calabrese served aboard two aircraft carriers, the USS *Enterprise* and USS *Bon Homme Richard*. His job was to ensure that the proper maintenance was performed on a single aircraft. "Each sailor was assigned to one plane," Calabrese explained. "I lived, ate, and sometimes slept, on that aircraft. I put in eighteen- to twenty-hour days at times. I strapped the pilot in before take-off and took him out when he returned. The pilot's life was in my hands. It was an awesome job for a nineteen-year-old kid like myself to be in charge of a multi-million dollar aircraft." Calabrese continued: "You had to be alert on the flight deck at all times. You literally faced death every day. You had to watch the cables, the bombs, and the fuel for the planes. Everything could be an accident waiting to happen. When I was aboard the *Bon Homme Richard*, I saw a guy get blown into the prop[eller] of a plane. He was killed instantly."

When the Vietnam War ended in 1973, twenty-one aircraft carriers had made eighty-six war cruises and spent 9,178 days in the Gulf of Tonkin. During this period, 377 Navy pilots were killed, 64 were listed as missing in action, and another 179 were captured when their aircraft were shot down.

## CRUISERS AND DESTROYERS

The Navy also had cruisers and destroyers stationed off the coast. The cruiser–destroyer group of the U.S. Seventh Fleet provided gunfire support to infantry units, training their huge guns on concentrations of enemy troops. Heavy cruisers

**Below:** The deafening 16-inch (406-millimeter) guns of the battleship USS *New Jersey* support U.S. Marines near the Demilitarized Zone (DMZ) in September 1968.

## TRAGEDY ABOARD THE USS *FORRESTAL*

Renowned insurance company Lloyd's of London called the flight deck on an aircraft carrier "the most dangerous four acres in the world." These words aptly describe the horrific accident that occurred on the USS *Forrestal* during the Vietnam War.

On Sunday morning, July 29, 1967, the *Forrestal* was conducting combat operations on Yankee Station in the Gulf of Tonkin. A Zuni missile was mistakenly launched from a stationary F-4 Phantom aircraft and ripped into the fuel tank of an A-4 Skyhawk fighter-bomber. A fire soon raged, which caused several additional explosions from other **ordnance** on the flight deck. By the time the inferno was finally extinguished, 134 crew members and Carrier Air Wing personnel were dead. Another 64 sailors of the 5,003-man crew had also sustained injuries.

Captain John K. Beling, the *Forrestal*'s commanding officer, later remarked: "I am most proud of the way the crew reacted. The thing that is foremost in my mind is the concrete demonstration that I have seen of the worth of American youth. I saw many examples of heroism. I saw, and subsequently heard of, not one single example of cowardice."

**Above:** Crew members assess the damage on the USS *Forrestal*. Flight deck operations could be extremely hazardous.

## THE GULF OF TONKIN INCIDENT

**Above:** A North Vietnamese torpedo boat is fired on by the destroyer USS *Maddox* during an incident that marked the beginning of the Vietnam War.

On August 2, 1964, while patrolling off the coast of North Vietnam, the destroyer USS *Maddox* was approached by three North Vietnamese Navy (NVN) torpedo boats. The three vessels ignored a warning shot and continued to close fast. The *Maddox* opened fire on the enemy boats. Four fighter jets from the USS *Ticonderoga* soon arrived and strafed the NVN boats. When it was over, one boat was stationary and on fire; the other two retreated. Two days later, the destroyer USS *C. Turner Joy* teamed up with the *Maddox* and returned to conduct surveillance of the enemy coastline. On the night of August 4, a radar operator aboard the *Maddox* picked up suspicious signals on the surface, and both ships opened fire in the direction of the mysterious signals. (Information obtained well after the fact indicates that there was actually no North Vietnamese attack that night. U.S. authorities were convinced at the time that one had taken place.) In light of these two events, President Lyndon B. Johnson asked Congress for a resolution to "take all necessary measures to repel an armed attack against the forces of the United States and to further prevent aggression." On August 7, 1964, Congress passed the Gulf of Tonkin Resolution. Some congressional members later said that they were misled and did not intend to give the president the go-ahead for a declaration of war. Congress later terminated the controversial resolution in 1970.

possessed 8-inch (203-mm) guns that had a range of 14 miles (22.5 km). The main **battery** could deliver up to 15 tons (13.6 tonnes) of shells on a selected target every minute. During its tours in Vietnam, the heavy cruiser USS *Newport News* fired almost eighty thousand rounds against enemy forces.

Destroyers had smaller, but no less deadly, 5-inch (127-mm) main guns that had a range of approximately 9 miles (14.5 km). "Naval shore bombardment is a highly skilled art, and we took great pride in laying the shells where they wanted," wrote

**Below:** Equipped with five cameras, an RF-8A Crusader reconnaissance aircraft is prepared for takeoff.

Commander Don Sheppard in *Destroyer Skipper, A Memoir of Command at Sea.*

To support the cruisers and destroyers, the Navy recommissioned the battleship USS *New Jersey.* The only battleship to serve in the Vietnam War, it arrived in September 1968 and immediately swung into action, firing its huge 16-inch (406-mm) guns in support of embattled U.S. Marines operating along the Demilitarized Zone (DMZ) that separated North and South Vietnam. The *New Jersey* fired two different rounds. One was a 2,700-pound (1,224-kilogram) armor-piercing shell that had a range of 21 miles (34 km) and could penetrate 30 feet (9 meters) of concrete. The other was a 1,900-pound (862-kg) projectile that could travel nearly 23 miles (37 km) to strike at enemy positions. The *Military Analysis Network* describes the procedure for preparing the round for firing: "The gunner and his numerous mates complete a carefully choreographed sequence of events, first sliding the projectile into the breech, then gingerly placing the cylindrical silk bags of black powder, then ratcheting the breech shut. An ominous red stripe on the wall of the turret just inches from the railing marks the boundary of the gun's recoil."

Fourteen Navy personnel earned the Medal of Honor for outstanding bravery during the Vietnam War. In all, 1,574 members of the Navy and Coast Guard were killed and nearly 10,000 were wounded. President Abraham Lincoln's words of praise for the Union Navy in the Civil War (1861–1865) apply to the Navy during the Vietnam War as well: "Nor must Uncle Sam's web feet be forgotten," he said. "At all the watery margins they have been present. Not only on the deep sea, the broad bay, and the rapid river, but also up the narrow muddy bayou and wherever the ground was a little damp, they have been and made their tracks."

## NAVAL AIR ACES OF THE WAR

**Left:** "Top Guns" Randy "Duke" Cunningham and William "Irish" Driscoll explain how they downed five MiG aircraft using only Sidewinder missiles in the skies over North Vietnam.

A military pilot is called an "ace" if he has shot down five or more enemy planes in enemy combat. On May 10, 1972, Lieutenant Randall J. Cunningham and Lieutenant junior grade (j.g.) William Driscoll became the first and only naval air aces of the Vietnam War, shooting down a North Vietnamese MiG-17 fighter over Haiphong. "The MiG was running!" described Robert Wilcox in his book *Scream of Eagles.* "Cunningham pulled hard, and they roared down after the MiG ... he fired ... he started to fire another Sidewinder when there was an abrupt burst of flame, black smoke, and the MiG flew to the ground. Cunningham pulled sharply up to avoid hitting the ground. They had gained their distinction in one of the longest sustained air battles of the war— approximately five minutes—and probably downed North Vietnam's best fighter pilot...."

# River Patrol

**Right:** A U.S. Navy patrol craft searches for enemy vessels in the "Parrot's Beak" area west of Saigon, during Operation Giant Slingshot in 1969.

During the Vietnam War, North Vietnam devised various methods to keep the flow of supplies and **materiel** moving into South Vietnam, so its army could continue to battle the United States and its allies. In addition to the Ho Chi Minh Trail, the communists used the South China Sea and the inland waterways to smuggle weapons, food, and ammunition. The U.S. Navy had the arduous task of attempting to stop this **contraband** from reaching the NVA and Viet Cong (VC) forces fighting in South Vietnam. The 1,200-mile (2,000-km) winding coastline and over 3,000 miles (5,000 km) of inland rivers and waterways posed a tremendous problem. Also, there were thousands of small fishing vessels, called **junks** or **sampans,** that could transport illegal cargo to the enemy.

## SWIFT BOATS

In March 1965, Operation Market Time was initiated. Its purpose was to intercept, seize, or destroy enemy boats in South Vietnam's coastal waters. It comprised numerous vessels, including radar picket destroyers, ocean and coastal minesweepers, U.S. and South Vietnamese Coast Guard cutters, small boats, and patrol aircraft to keep a watchful eye on the coast.

A 50-foot (15-m) snub-nosed vessel, designated Patrol Craft, Fast (PCF), was employed to patrol South Vietnam's shallow coastal waters. The sailors referred to them as Swift Boats, or just Swifts. The crew consisted of one officer and five enlisted men. A lieutenant junior grade (j.g.) was in command of the boat. A boatswain's mate was in charge of the operational maintenance and upkeep of the ship. The engineman spent long hours maintaining the boat's motors in what the crew called the "snipe locker." A gunner's mate repaired and cleaned all the vessel's weapons. Usually, a deckhand was on board to give assistance. The small boats were powered by two diesel engines and could reach a top speed of 28 knots, or 32 miles (51 km) per hour. They were also heavily armed with machine guns and a wide variety of rifles, pistols, and grenade launchers.

## THE PBR

In December 1965, the Navy began Operation Game Warden to cut the enemy supply lines on the rivers and inland waterways. The boats and personnel involved in the operation have been commonly referred to as the Brown Water Navy, because the rivers of Vietnam were a muddy brown color. The Patrol Boat, River (PBR) was specially designed for this difficult mission. The 31-foot (9.5-m) craft had a pair of water jets that enabled the vessel to

**Below:** A U.S. Navy patrol boat races up the My Tho River, one of the main tributaries of the Mekong Delta, in June 1969.

**Left:** The young crew of this Swift Boat, pictured on the Mekong Delta, includes future U.S. Senator and Democratic Party presidential nominee John Kerry (far right).

move through extremely shallow water at a top speed of 30 knots, or 35 miles (56 km) per hour. The boat was highly susceptible to damage by enemy fire, however, because of its fiberglass hull. Later, the newer PBRs had aluminum covering for added protection. PBRs had a crew of only four, but they were heavily armed. Unlike the Swifts, there was no commissioned officer in charge. Usually, an enlisted first class petty officer was in command, with an engineman, gunner's mate, and seaman. PBRs possessed high-quality radar and communications equipment, which was essential because the majority of their operations were conducted after nightfall. These included Sea, Air, and Land (SEAL) team insertions, night ambushes, and suspected enemy vessel searches.

Life aboard the Swift Boats and PBRs could, at times, be nerve-racking. In his book, *Brown Water, Black Berets*, author Lieutenant Commander Tom Cutler describes the life of a sailor: "The young

## SEAWOLVES AND BLACK PONIES

Since the PBRs were so vulnerable, additional protection, in the form of airpower, was needed. The Navy, however, had no attack helicopters. That dilemma was soon solved when the Army and the Navy entered a joint service agreement. The Army lent twenty-two UH-1B Iroquois (Huey) helicopters for use in Operation Game Warden. In June 1967, the unit was designated Helicopter Attack (Light) Squadron Three, or HAL-3. They called themselves the Seawolves. Although the Navy had other combat helicopters, this was the only rapid-reaction attack-helicopter squadron ever commissioned in the Navy.

Flying along the twisting rivers and canals was a difficult job. The helicopters had to skim the treetops and get in close to provide fire support for the PBRs. To supplement the Seawolves, a fixed-wing squadron was formed in January 1969. Light Attack Squadron Four (VAL–4) consisted of fourteen OV–10A Broncos, a twin-engine, propeller-driven plane with a high tail boom. It was outfitted with machine guns, a Gatling-type mini-gun, and small and large rocket pods. The Black Ponies, as the pilots who flew these fixed-wing aircraft called themselves, always flew in pairs. A night maneuver, known as chumming, was developed to ferret out the enemy. One Bronco flew with all its lights on, acting as a decoy. Just above was a second plane in complete darkness. If enemy contact was made, the aircraft flying at the higher altitude immediately swooped down to eliminate the threat.

sailor was in a distant land he had only recently heard of to help the Vietnamese people, yet he could never trust any of them. He was there to preserve their freedom, yet he had to intrude upon their private lives, rummaging through their possessions. The nature of the war and of his occupation dictated that he must view every Vietnamese as a potential friend and, at the same time, as a deadly enemy."

In a February 1996 interview in *Vietnam Magazine*, Radioman Third Class Raul Herrera, a Market Time sailor in Swift Boats, described a typical boarding operation: "You had to be careful. The fishing junks and sampans were scattered in certain locations

**Above:** A U.S. Navy special operations SEAL talks with a Seawolf pilot about an upcoming mission.

**Above:** A Swift Boat sailor in 1968 waves a greeting. Crews had to be alert on patrol. Boredom could be quickly replaced by moments of sheer terror.

of each patrol area. We would conduct inspections of these boats on a random basis. Most of the junks and sampans were occupied by older fishermen trying to catch enough fish so their families could survive, or to sell at the village market. Weapons were often sealed in tubular canisters and secured to the junks' undersides. So we would drag a rope along the bottom of the junks' **keel** to check for contraband. The transiting cargo vessels, on the other hand, always required on-board inspections. They were capable of carrying large containers, which they usually filled with rice. We used a metal detector rod to probe the containers and check for weapons."

Brown Water Navy sailors had dangerous jobs. Paul Cagle was a crew member of PBR-139 when his vessel was struck by enemy fire on January 31, 1969, as it patrolled the Vam Co Dong River. His narrative illustrates the harrowing combat PBR sailors experienced in Vietnam: "One minute everything was calm," he wrote, "except for the gentle hum of the engines. Then from the corner of my eye, I saw a white sparkle. This was followed by a deafening explosion that literally blew me into the air about 10 feet (3 m) above the boat. I could not hear anything and time was in slow motion, but I remember the green **tracers** going by me."

By war's end, nearly one thousand men who had served aboard the PBRs, Swift Boats, and other riverine vessels, had been killed in action. Because of their heroism and devotion to duty, these brave sailors have reserved their rightful place in Navy history.

# WHITE GHOSTS: THE U.S. COAST GUARD

Although the Coast Guard falls under the jurisdiction of the Department of Transportation, the president of the United States can direct it to assist the Navy during time of war. In 1965, the Coast Guard was ordered to operate with the Navy in Operation Market Time. Twenty-six Coast Guard patrol boats were soon off the coast of South Vietnam. Painted white, instead of the usual Navy gray, they were called White Ghosts by the enemy.

Besides its sea duties, the Coast Guard had security officers and explosives-loading detachments to oversee the unloading of ammunition, bombs, and other dangerous cargo in South Vietnamese ports. It provided Long Range Aids to Navigation (LORAN) to maintain security and to ensure vessels navigated the harbors safely. In addition, it administered humanitarian aid to the civilian population. Coast Guard helicopter pilots flew with Air Force personnel on search-and-rescue missions.

The Coast Guard had an impressive record in the war. Its personnel boarded nearly 250,000 junks and sampans and took part in 6,000 naval gunfire missions. Seven Coastguardsmen died in Vietnam and another fifty-three were wounded.

**Below:** Coast Guard vessel *Point Clear* patrols off the coast of South Vietnam. It served from July 1965 until September 1969.

# Navy SEALs

**Right:** Navy SEALs demolish a Viet Cong bunker in the Mekong Delta, January 14, 1969.

In January 1962, the Navy decided to form its own special-warfare group, calling its operatives SEALs, an acronym for Sea-Air-Land. SEALs could infiltrate behind enemy lines by sea in small boats or underwater, by air from a helicopter or parachute, and by land as part of normal patrolling. All of these methods enabled them to collect intelligence, capture an enemy soldier, or perform other acts of sabotage as directed.

## SEAL TRAINING

SEAL commandos went through rigorous training known as the Basic Underwater Demolition/SEAL course, or simply BUDS. The training was separated into three phases. Phase One relied heavily on physical training and getting the recruits into shape. Phase two concentrated on diving techniques. Phase three focused on demolition and land-warfare training. If the sailor successfully completed the eighteen-week school, he earned the right to wear the distinctive SEAL emblem—an eagle clutching an anchor and trident.

## SEALS IN VIETNAM

SEALs began arriving in Vietnam in 1965. They mainly operated in the Mekong Delta and the Rung Sat Special Zone (RSSZ), a swampy delta of the Saigon and Dong Nai Rivers. They operated in teams, and there were never more than fourteen teams in Vietnam at any one time. There were only 350 SEALs available during the Vietnam War, but despite their small numbers, SEALs made a tremendous impact. Their clandestine

**Below:** Rappelling from helicopters was just one method SEALs used to infiltrate behind enemy lines.

## THE PHOENIX PROGRAM

The objective of the Phoenix Program was to identify the estimated seven hundred VC political leaders and other high-ranking communists who had organized thousands of assassinations, bombings, and other acts of terror against the South Vietnamese government. Among the Phoenix program's members were a small number of Navy SEALs. Their main assignment was either to capture or kill high-level VC leaders. The SEALs received assistance from the South Vietnamese Police Provisional Reconnaissance Unit (PRU) and naval intelligence-gathering liaison officers. Although controversial, the Phoenix Program was deemed a tremendous success. Even the communists admitted this after the war. The program eliminated many VC bases within South Vietnam, and the assassinations carried out by SEALs and other program members were effective in eroding support for the VC in many areas.

**Above:** A member of U.S. Navy Seal Team One wears camouflage grease paint to blend into the jungles of South Vietnam.

**Left:** A SEAL crouches at the front of a small patrol craft, his M16 rifle at the ready.

operations were so successful that they became particularly feared by the enemy, who referred to them as "men with green faces" because of the camouflage paint they wore while on patrol. SEALs often used the element of surprise to strike at larger enemy forces. While patrolling on riverboats in the RSSZ during 1968, one six-man SEAL team encountered a rear-guard security group for two VC battalions. Instead of retreating, the men waded ashore and drove the enemy back with heavy automatic weapons fire. Although numerically superior, the VC thought they had run into a bigger unit and quickly retreated into the jungle.

Sometimes SEALs had to rely on their training and skills to avoid a disaster. One such incident occurred in 1968 when a SEAL team became involved in an intense firefight with an

**Right:** A SEAL watches the shoreline through the sight on a recoilless rifle while on patrol in the Rung Sat Special Zone.

estimated 550- to 600-man VC unit. Although peppered with **shrapnel**, SEAL Robert Gallagher, using his rifle as a crutch, organized a defensive perimeter to protect the Landing Zone (LZ). Every SEAL maintained his discipline and killed numerous enemy soldiers attempting to breach their lines. Helicopters arrived in time to extract the beleaguered men. Gallagher was presented the Navy Cross, the nation's second-highest award, for his exemplary bravery that night.

The SEALs were unique during the Vietnam War. They performed many tasks and were feared by the enemy. In *Never Fight Fair: Navy SEALs' Stories of Combat and Adventure*, author Orr Kelly describes them in this manner: "They really, really, really want to go into life-threatening, extremely dangerous situations. They want to go up to Father Death and look him right square in the face and give him a knockout punch in the eye."

## "THE FOREST OF ASSASSINS"

The area adjacent to the Long Tau River, on which the important port of Saigon was situated, was known as the Rung Sat Special Zone (RSSZ). Its ominous English translation is "Killer Forest" or "Forest of Assassins." In this marshy area of mangrove swamps, the Viet Cong tried to interrupt the flow of supplies to the Saigon government. Among the various units assigned to protect this vital river were the SEALs.

## SEAL MEDAL OF HONOR

In the pre-dawn hours of October 31, 1972, a small inflatable boat quietly came ashore at the Cua Viet River near the Demilitarized Zone (DMZ). The rubber craft was carrying a five-man SEAL team. Their mission was to capture an NVA officer and collect intelligence on an enemy river base nearby. The team leader, Lieutenant Thomas R. Norris, was already recommended for the Medal of Honor, having successfully rescued two downed U.S. pilots in April. Hiding their craft, the men secretly made their way through the sand dunes. The mission was uneventful until the men were spotted by enemy soldiers. A firefight ensued, and additional NVA soldiers arrived, trapping the SEALs. Supported by naval gunfire from offshore, the besieged men fought tenaciously, but the NVA, despite the covering fire, crawled to within 25 yards (22 m) of their position. Norris ordered his men to retreat to the sea to be rescued. During the withdrawal, however, Norris was seriously wounded in the head. Determined not to leave him, SEAL Michael E. Thornton sprinted through enemy gunfire to retrieve Norris. Despite bleeding from both legs as a result of shrapnel wounds, Thornton carried Norris into the water, inflated his life jacket, and swam until they were out of range of the NVA fire. For two hours, Thornton swam with Norris until they were picked up by a Vietnamese junk. Both men survived. Thornton earned the Medal of Honor for his courageous efforts that night. This incident is the only one in which a Medal of Honor recipient saved another Medal of Honor recipient's life in combat.

# U.S. Marines

**Right:** Infantrymen of the Third Marine Division land at Red Beach in Da Nang, South Vietnam, on March 8, 1965.

The Marine Corps' primary role prior to the Vietnam War was amphibious assaults on enemy beachheads. Although the Marines performed such a role in Vietnam with the Special Landing Force (SLF), they also fought a protracted land war, much like the Army. The Marines were in South Vietnam in the 1950s in advisory roles to the newly formed South Vietnamese Marine Corps. Also, in 1962, a Marine helicopter squadron participated in Operation Shufly in support of the Army of the Republic of Vietnam (ARVN). It wasn't until March 1965, however, that the Marines arrived in South Vietnam in force. Elements of the Third Marine Division waded ashore at Red Beach in Da Nang and flew into Chu Lai, just south of Da Nang. Their primary purpose was to provide security for the two airfields at each location. That purpose was soon to change.

## MARINE OPERATIONS

In August 1965, Lieutenant General Lewis W. "Silent Lew" Walt, commanding general of the Third Marine Amphibious Force (III MAF), received reports from a captured VC soldier that the First VC Regiment was preparing to assault Chu Lai Airfield. Walt decided to gamble on attacking the VC first. While the Fourth Marines were flown into three landing zones, dubbed Red, White, and Blue, the Third Marines would hit the beach on the Van Tuong Peninsula. The two units would then close together, trapping the VC between them. The operation was code-named Starlite and was the first large-scale operation of the Vietnam War. On August 18, 1965, the Third Marines disembarked from their landing craft and quickly moved inland to link up with the Fourth Marines. Meanwhile, helicopters ferried the Fourth Marines to their destinations. The situation on Landing Zone Blue took a turn for the worse, however. The Marines had landed on top of a VC battalion headquarters. As soon as the infantrymen leaped from the choppers, enemy gunfire snapped and cracked around them. Quickly reorganizing, the riflemen called in air strikes and artillery on enemy positions. As these enemy positions were eliminated, the Marines pressed forward.

Two Marines earned the Medal of Honor that day. Lance Corporal Joe C. Paul kept the enemy from advancing while his wounded comrades were evacuated. Even after he was struck by enemy fire, Paul remained in his position until he died. Corporal Robert O'Malley was wounded three times while eliminating enemy soldiers in spider holes—small dugouts in which one soldier could hide. O'Malley was everywhere on the battlefield. He refused medical treatment until all his squad members were evacuated. Starlite was deemed a major success. This first major encounter between the two adversaries set the stage for future combat operations. Throughout 1966 and 1967, the Marines participated in many search-and-destroy operations. Marine aircraft and helicopters flew thousands of **sorties** to assist the infantry during this period.

## THE TET OFFENSIVE

In early 1968, the NVA and Viet Cong planned a major offensive in South Vietnam. It coincided with the biggest Vietnamese holiday, known as Tet, or New Year. Every major city was under attack. On January 21, 1968, the NVA crossed the DMZ and attacked the Marines at the Khe Sanh Combat Base near the Laotian border. An estimated 30,000 to 40,000 NVA surrounded the small, isolated outpost. Marines withstood constant artillery barrages as well as hand-to-hand fighting. To keep the NVA from overrunning Khe Sanh, Operation Niagara was initiated. Utilizing electronic sensors along the DMZ, fighter-bombers flew about 24,000 air strikes, and B-52 bombers chalked up another 2,700 sorties. An average of 300 air strikes were sent to Khe Sanh every day. Every hour and a half, three B-52s dropped their bomb load, as close as 300 yards (275 m) from the Marine perimeter. Over 110,000 pounds (50,000 kg) of ordnance was dropped in and around the combat base. "There were so many bomb craters it looked like the surface of the moon," remarked one Marine. The siege of Khe Sanh ended in early April. The Marines had endured seventy-seven days of horrific combat. More than 200 lost their lives and hundreds more were wounded. The NVA was estimated to have sustained between 10,000 and 15,000 casualties.

The ancient imperial capital of Hue, located on Highway One, halfway between Da Nang and the DMZ, was the scene of brutal

**Below:** A Marine keeps his head low as he drags his buddy from the ruins of the citadel in the city of Hue in 1968.

**Above:** Marines read a magazine during a break in the street fighting in Hue during the 1968 Tet Offensive.

fighting during the Tet Offensive. Communist soldiers assaulted the city, and for the next month, Marines had to drive them out. Much of the combat was house-to-house. By early March, Hue had been retaken. The NVA and VC fled. It wasn't until the following year, however, that a horrible discovery was made. The communists had murdered many of the civilians.

As military historian Eric Hammel notes in *Fire in the Streets: The Battle for Hue, 1968,* "The real tragedy of the battle for Hue lay, not in the physical damage or even the loss of national treasures, but in the deaths of many hundreds of Hue's citizens—the random deaths and maimings in the battles to liberate the city, and in the nearly 2,000 documented cases of mass murder and execution that claimed the lives of many of the nation's leading businessmen, government workers, politicians, theologians, foreign missionaries and doctors, intellectuals, and teachers."

Fifty-seven Medals of Honor were awarded to Marines during the Vietnam War. But the cost was high. In the end, over 13,000 were killed in action and nearly 88,000 were wounded. Every Marine who served with honor during the Vietnam War lived up to their motto, *Semper Fidelis*, Latin for "Always Faithful."

# THE COMBINED ACTION PROGRAM

Marines were innovators in another field during the war: pacification. They developed plans to provide security for local villages by training members of the Vietnamese Popular Forces (PFs) and Regional Forces (RFs), akin to the National Guard. If these individuals could be trained in squad tactics and firearms, and instilled with pride and discipline, the Marines felt, then they could defend their own villages. Marine squads were assigned to villages to train the PFs and RFs under the Combined Action Program (CAP). The program reached its height in 1970 with the Marines contributing forty-two officers and about two thousand enlisted men.

**Above:** Marines not only trained the South Vietnamese villagers in squad tactics, they also took care of their medical needs.

Being a CAP Marine was not easy. While most soldiers just passed through the villages, CAP Marines lived, ate, worked, and fought alongside their Vietnamese counterparts. The key to the success of the program was the bond between members of the two forces, who often became close partners in dangerous situations. Rocky Jay was a CAP Marine in 1969. One night, his patrol was ambushed, and he later recalled: "As I lay there bleeding in the mud with the rain hitting me in the face, one of the PFs was crawling around on his hands and knees. He saw me and crawled over to me. I saw that he'd suffered a horrible head wound. He wiped my face and lay down next to me. I don't even remember the guy's name. I should know his name." To this day, Jay does not know the fate of the, PF wounded.

# The Tragic End

**Right:** With the surrender of Da Nang imminent, South Vietnamese civilians are evacuated by the U.S. Navy on March 24, 1975.

After eight years of bloody combat, the United States and North Vietnam signed the Paris Peace Accord on January 27, 1973. By the end of March, the Military Assistance Command, Vietnam (MACV) was dissolved and replaced by the Defense Attaché Office (DAO). Only a few naval personnel remained. The Marines had five officers and 140 enlisted men in the Security Guard Battalion. By early summer, that number was reduced to 90. Most of these Marines were scattered throughout South Vietnam, performing protection and administrative duties at the embassy and **consulates**. Both the communists and the Army of the Republic of Vietnam (ARVN), however, violated the peace treaty, and the fighting continued. By the end of 1974, the NVA had gained footholds, but remained cautious because of the ever-looming threat of American air superiority.

## THE END LOOMS NEAR

The North Vietnamese then chose a risky move. They decided to attack Phuoc Long Province, just 75 miles (120 km) north of Saigon, to test the Americans. By January 6, 1975, the communists had seized the entire province. Inactivity by the United States prompted the North Vietnamese to speed up the timetable for the complete takeover of the country.

By mid-March, South Vietnamese president Nguyen Van Thieu ordered his commanders to **cede** all of the Central Highlands to the NVA. He then had the elite ARVN Airborne Division withdraw to protect Saigon. These two disastrous decisions precipitated the end of South Vietnam. In less than ten days, the NVA had control of half the country and had begun to close in on Da Nang. While the defenses around the key port of Da Nang crumbled, the Marine security guard, led by Staff Sergeant Walter W. Sparks, relocated to the U.S. Consulate. Here, they shredded

**Right:** U.S. service personnel in Da Nang are forced to take cover as North Vietnamese artillery shells explode nearby on January 26, 1975.

and destroyed classified material before their departure. Albert A. Francis, the consulate general, moved the staff to a prearranged landing zone for evacuation by helicopter. It was learned, however, that no helicopters would be coming. Air America, the cover name for aircraft operated by the Central Intelligence Agency (CIA), had expended all its fuel, and the South

Vietnamese had refused its request for more. Since Da Nang was a coastal city, it was decided that the safest method of travel was by tugboat or barge because the roads were now congested with thousands of refugees escaping the communist invasion.

In the pre-dawn hours of March 29, 1975, Sparks and his men rode in a covered garbage truck to the pier, where the boats were waiting. As they leaped from the vehicle to get on board the vessels, they encountered South Vietnamese civilians also attempting to flee Da Nang by boat. Sparkes recalled the disturbing events that transpired: "We got off the truck and helped the people on this barge. That…was one of the most tragic things I have seen in my life, and I have been in combat a few times…Women and old people were throwing their babies to that barge for people to catch, and they were missing and falling in the

**Below:** While the Eighteenth ARVN Division defends Xuan Loc from the advancing communist forces, residents of the city board a U.S. helicopter to fly to safety on April 14, 1975.

water. Old people crawling up this rope, trying to get to the
barge and falling off, and then the barge would come back
and crush them."

As the Americans fled Da Nang, thousands of planes, tanks,
and armored vehicles, along with tons of ammunition and
supplies, were abandoned. The NVA rolled into the city and
captured it on March 30, 1975. There was no resistance to the
communist takeover.

## THE MOVEMENT TO TAKE SAIGON

In April, the enemy consolidated its forces and prepared to move
on the grand prize, the capital city of South Vietnam, Saigon. The
communists ran into stiff resistance at Xuan Loc 40 miles (64 km)
northeast of Saigon. The Eighteenth ARVN Division fought
bravely, holding off repeated NVA assaults. On April 9, however,
the enemy overran Xuan Loc. With the enemy momentum
moving rapidly toward Saigon, thousands of civilians clogged the
roads, trying to make it to the capital and escape South Vietnam
with U.S. help. Many of these individuals, unfortunately, were
greatly disappointed and did not manage to escape.

The USS *Durham*, an amphibious cargo ship, began to take
refugees on board while it was docked in Cam Ranh Bay, 180
miles (290 km) northeast of Saigon. Soon, other ships from the
Military Sealift Command (MSC) arrived to pick up South
Vietnamese and transport them to Phu Quoc Island, off the
western coast of South Vietnam in the Gulf of Thailand. Marines
were put on board to provide security. Thirty-thousand South
Vietnamese naval personnel, their families, and civilians were
eventually rescued by sea.

Meanwhile, Navy and Marine planners were organizing the
evacuation of the DAO. Called the Special Planning Group
(SPG), they chose a three-phase plan. First, all the South

## LAST STAND AT THE EMBASSY

With the departure of Ambassador Graham Martin from the embassy on April 30, 1975, a handful of Marines were still waiting to be evacuated. Major James H. Kean, officer in charge of the Security Guard Detachment, had ten men with him. They barricaded the front door to the building and raced to the top of the embassy to be in close proximity to the landing zone when the rescue helicopter arrived. Angry because they had been left behind, some South Vietnamese began to open fire on the contingent of Marines. Civilians broke through the doors and tried to reach the rooftop where Kean and his men were situated. Kean and the men lobbed tear gas canisters to hold them off. To their relief, a CH-46 set down just before eight o'clock in the morning to bring them to safety. It was the last American helicopter to leave the country.

**Left:** South Vietnamese refugees gather outside the U.S. Embassy trying to gain entry for a flight to freedom. Additional Marines were flown into Saigon to man the walls for crowd control.

**Above:** CIA helicopter lands on a rooftop at 22 Gia Long Street in Saigon to evacuate waiting civilians.

Vietnamese who had collaborated with the Americans would be removed. The incoming North Vietnamese would almost certainly execute them. Second was the relocation of all individuals from Saigon and the embassy to the DAO compound. The last phase was the final extraction of all personnel from the DAO compound. The whole operation was dubbed Frequent Wind.

"We had to devise a plan to fortify and reinforce the compound to hold ten thousand people for ten days should the situation dictate that in order to accomplish evacuation," explained Captain Anthony A. Wood. "Immediately I called it 'the Alamo' because it seemed obvious that was what we were doing, and the name stuck." Wood assisted in planning the evacuation routes for people going from downtown Saigon to the DAO. He used names taken from the geography of the American West, such as Oregon, Santa Fe, and Texas, for the routes. Because of this, his fellow officers referred to him as "the wagon master."

## SAIGON FALLS

On April 29, the NVA began shelling Saigon. After assessing the damage, the U.S. Ambassador to South Vietnam, Graham Martin, phoned Secretary of State Henry Kissinger to brief him. At 10:51 A.M., Brigadier General Richard A. Carey, assistant commander of the First Marine Air Wing, received word to commence Operation Frequent Wind. The end was near.

The USS *Coral Sea* and USS *Enterprise* were situated off the coast to provide close-air support. Helicopters from ships of the MSC in the South China Sea began the evacuation of personnel from the DAO. Carey, however, received an urgent call from the embassy explaining that more than two thousand people were waiting to be airlifted from the DAO. The embassy compound, about 5 miles (8 km) northwest of the DAO, was originally abandoned as a landing zone because it was too small. Now, Carey had no other option. He had to get those individuals out of there. Carey quickly shifted 130 Marines to the embassy to bolster its defenses against the hordes of civilians outside the gates. CH-53 and CH-46 helicopters were instantly dispatched to pick up the crowd of people awaiting their flight to safety. By ten o'clock that night, the DAO airlift was successfully finished. Amid the

**Below:** The end comes. On April 30, 1975, NVA troops break through the gates of the Presidential Palace in Saigon as the city falls to the communists.

explosions of **thermite grenades** launched by the NVA, the last pair of helicopters took off from the DAO. Aboard the command ship USS *Blue Ridge*, Brigadier General Carey and his staff shifted their full attention to the embassy.

A makeshift landing zone was hastily established in the embassy courtyard to land the larger CH-53 helicopters. Marines guarded the walls to block any more civilians from entering the compound. Soon, another landing zone was set up at the Combined Recreation Association (CRA) area nearby. As the situation grew tense, efforts were made to calm the crowd,

**Below:** A helicopter is pushed from a carrier deck into the sea during Operation Frequent Wind to make room for additional aircraft.

reassuring them that all would be flown to safety. South Vietnamese Air Force (SVNAF) pilots, accompanied by their families, flew their planes to ships off the coast. Forty-one of these made emergency landings in the ocean, but all the passengers were recovered by the Navy. Another fifty-four aircraft landed on board, but had to be pushed over the side by crewmembers so U.S. helicopters could continue to evacuate individuals from Saigon. Every ten minutes a helicopter landed at the embassy. Ambassador Martin tried to get as many South Vietnamese out as possible. "It appeared to be a bottomless pit," said Vice Admiral George P. Steele. "I did not want him (Ambassador Martin) captured. Through loyalty to our Vietnamese colleagues, he was going to keep that evacuation going indefinitely, and in my opinion, force it to keep going by not coming out himself."

Finally, just before dawn on April 30, 1975, Ambassador Martin was lifted from the embassy. Operation Frequent Wind, despite all its complexities, was a tremendous success. Pilots logged over 680 sorties. Only two helicopters were lost. Nearly 5,000 people were removed from the DAO and another 978 U.S. citizens and over 1,100 others were removed from the American embassy. Later that same day, NVA troops entered Saigon. South Vietnamese president General Tran Van Minh, who had assumed control when President Thieu resigned weeks earlier, surrendered. The Vietnam War was finally over.

## THE LAST MARINES KILLED IN VIETNAM

At 4:00 A.M., on April 29, 1975, NVA rockets slammed into Tan Son Nhut Air Base, about a mile west of the DAO. One rocket landed just 6 feet (2 m) from the building. Fourteen people were thrown from their beds, but, miraculously, none were hurt. Two U.S. Marines guarding a roadblock near Gate Four of the DAO compound were killed instantly when several projectiles exploded near their position. Corporal Charles McMahon, Jr., of Woburn, Massachusetts, and Lance Corporal Darwin D. Judge of Marshalltown, Iowa, were the last Marines to die in Vietnam.

# Time Line

**1955:** October, South Vietnam officially becomes the Republic of Vietnam (RVN).

**1962:** Military Assistance Command, Vietnam (MACV) is established in Saigon.

**1964:** August, USS *Maddox* is reportedly attacked by North Vietnamese in Gulf of Tonkin; Congress passes the Gulf of Tonkin Resolution; July, U.S. Navy begins monitoring junk and sampan traffic off the coast of North Vietnam.

**1965:** May, Operation Market Time begins; July, first U.S. Coast Guard cutters arrive in RVN; December, Operation Game Warden begins.

**1966:** March, first Seawolf helicopters arrive in RVN.

**1967:** Navy begins Mobile Riverine Force operations in the Rung Sat Special Zone (RSSZ).

**1968:** January, Tet Offensive is launched.

**1969:** January, Light Attack Squadron is commissioned for duty in South Vietnam to support the Brown Water Navy; 250,000 march in antiwar demonstration in Washington, D.C.

**1970:** Widespread demonstrations protest the war; December, Congress repeals the Gulf of Tonkin Resolution.

**1972:** December, President Nixon orders B-52s to strike at targets in North Vietnam.

**1973:** January, peace accords are signed in Paris, France; March, last U.S. ground troops leave Vietnam.

**1975:** January, North Vietnam announces an all-out offensive to seize South Vietnam; April, last U.S. citizens are evacuated from Saigon; North Vietnamese take Saigon the next day.

# Glossary

**artillery:** large-caliber guns operated by a crew

**battalion:** a military unit composed of a headquarters and two or more companies or batteries

**battery:** a grouping of artillery pieces

**cede:** to yield or grant

**consulate:** the office of an official appointed by a state to live in a foreign city and protect the state's citizens and interests there

**contraband:** goods or merchandise whose importation, exportation, or possession is forbidden

**guerrilla:** a person who engages in irregular warfare, especially as a member of an independent unit carrying out harrassment or sabotage

**junk:** flat-bottomed sailing vessel used in Southeast Asia and China

**keel:** the lengthwise timber or steel structure running along the bottom of a ship

**materiel:** military equipment, apparatus, and supplies

**ordnance:** bombs, shells, or other ammunition

**sampan:** small boat propelled by an oar or oars at the stern, common in Southeast Asia and China

**shrapnel:** fragments thrown out by an explosion

**sortie:** an operational flight by a single aircraft

**thermite grenade:** an explosive device containing aluminum powder and iron oxide and which burns at a very high temperature

**tracer:** a round of ammunition whose course is visible in flight

# Further Reading

## BOOKS

**Corbett, John.** *West Dickens Avenue: A Marine at Khe Sanh.*
New York: Ballantine Books, 2003.

**Cutler, Thomas J.** *Brown Water, Black Berets: Coastal and Riverine
Warfare in Vietnam.* Annapolis, MD: Naval Institute Press, 2000.

**Fawcett, Bill (Editor).** *Hunters and Shooters: An Oral History of the
U.S. Navy SEALs in Vietnam.* New York: William Morrow, 1995.

**Goldsmith, Wynn.** *Papa Bravo Romeo: U.S. Navy Patrol Boats at
War in Vietnam.* New York: Ballantine Books, 2001.

**Larzelere, Alex.** *The Coast Guard at War: Vietnam, 1965–1975.*
Annapolis, MD: Naval Institute Press, 1997.

## WEB SITES

### The U.S. Navy Historical Center
www.history.navy.mil/
*The Navy keeps an extensive archive of historical information online.*

### The Riverine Navy in Vietnam
www.vietvet.org/rbruder.htm
*Holds accounts of operations by U.S. Naval Forces in Vietnam.*

### "By Sea, Air, and Land"
www.history.navy.mil/seairland/
*This is a history of the U.S. Navy in Southeast Asia.*

### The Navy in Vietnam
www.bcres.com/benewah/navymenu.htm
*Provides an overview of the various naval activities in the Vietnam War.*

# Index